The Garden in Winter and Other Poems

University of Texas Press Poetry Series, No. 7

The Garden in Winter and Other Poems

BY PRENTISS MOORE

University of Texas Press, Austin

Publication of this book was assisted by the Maher
Contingency Fund.

First Edition, 1981

Library of Congress Cataloging in Publication Data
Moore, Prentiss, 1947–
   The garden in winter and other poems.
   (University of Texas Press poetry series; no. 7)
   I. Title. II. Series.
PS3563.O627G3   811'.54   81-13117
ISBN 0-292-72721-6   AACR2
ISBN 0-292-72722-4 (pbk.)

For Gordon and Robert

Contents

and headlong into the dark pool he fell
as when some flaming star falls
from the heavens headlong into the sea,
and some sailor cries to his comrades,
"Make your tackle snug, my lads;
it is a sailing breeze."

Theocritus XIII

I still remember the first time I used a pattern language in this way. I found myself so completely caught up in the process that I was trembling. A handful of simple statements made it possible for my mind to flow out and open, through them—and yet, although the house which came was made by me, born of my feelings, it was at the same time as though the house became real, almost by itself, of its own volition, through my thoughts.

It is a fearsome thing, like diving into water. And yet it is exhilarating—because you aren't controlling it. You are only the medium in which the patterns come to life, and of their own accord give birth to something new.

Christopher Alexander
The Timeless Way of Building

The Garden in Winter and Other Poems

Constellation

The beautiful high relief by
della Robbia in Florence
of a small boys' choir . . .

it is not that music is
being denoted through the silence
of the medium, or even

the relative subtlety of the
gesture, eyes trained together
and mouths open, but the boys'

closeness to each other,
almost paradoxical in beings
otherwise so given to

diversion and play.

Romance on Reading Meng Chiao's "Sadness of the Gorges"

Time when we are most to ourselves.
White on white. One masking zero.
Faint thunder ranges in the sky.
This is the abstract, distinct
from all else, flesh from bone,
the fragment which the old see
everywhere, the field in mist.
We ask if sensation is weakness,
if there is "a providential correspondence
between truth and human need."
Though we cannot believe our words,
which are incantation, Ouroboros,
'absence is the presence of presence,'
the words like scales grasping the earth,
a shape of power, and how we live
with them if life is not only
words. We need not tease the
little sparrows, or unnerve the sun
to see how things go. Here on the page
the letters' minuteness records
"the frost perches mournful
cadences, remote and clear." Detail
is the scattered knowledge of things.
It is not the knowledge of desire,
or the hypnotic onus of its denial.

On Climbing the Big Pagoda in Changan
AFTER TU FU

The wind drums without end here
where one might at last
step out into the sky.
It is not only the fear of height
one feels. This is the power
of Buddha made external,
crannies between dragon
and serpent revealing the intricacies
of construction, support
and span marking the Milky Way.
The clear autumn moon tries to come
into view, but clouds shatter the
pattern of mountains, and
clear Wei and muddy Ching mingle
in one final mist obscuring
the whole kingdom. One cries from
unknown depth for Shun to awaken.
But alas, by Jade Lake the Fairy
Queen Mother takes her wine,
and earth is folded into this darkness.
The yellow cranes cannot end their
aimless flight. And into the
setting sun silent wild geese stream
without knowing, impelled to life.

Map

Ever. The word ever. As in the
Psalms, will He ever

hear, that dread that
the obstruction is oneself . . .

will the flesh ever resume its place
on Grandmother's bones

or the self
bless itself . . .

one contemplates the end trying to
discover the propriety, the

passage to China,
uncharted,

where are set the decorative
coils of a monster

never quite brought
into time

Signature

Ice in the trees. Last
night, or the night before

suicide of the lover of
my friend. We talked later.

My friend said "abundance"
though he explained there was "so

much more life, people,
than could ever possibly

realize itself by
its standards," that it "seems more

directed by quantity
than quality." He said

we didn't know
where how we feel about

ourselves comes from,
"though the obvious thing

is that it's passed on from
other people." He said we'd

have to become more Buddhist,
or passive, about it.

He complained only that it
was when he had to use

words that he was
overwhelmed by the feeling.

I thought of
Gordon's distinction,

that prose is how the language keeps
on, whereas poetry is how

the words freeze, and Williams
saying that prose in

the end is emotional
as poetry is not,

like psychosis,
where emotion drops

out between the thought
and the feeling,

which I understood only
when I read a

verse of Kikaku, about moonlight in
freezing stillness on the

great locked bolt
of a door.

I walked home noticing
the ice on bushes and

trees, how especially
on the clustered leaves it

clarified something about
their form, an accentuation,

though still unassimilated,
as a signature begins

to become illegible by its
very identity.

A History of Style

"That universal prose that speaks
of itself to all men . . ."

The barbarian in one lashes
out at the

new god,
and only

with resentment,
and only because he has an

instinct to survive
anywhere,

consigns himself
to that barren room

where his flesh will wither
and skin turn pale

and he will find out how to banish even
the word,

never understanding his fierce,
undying

love for the mind's dark,
dark humility.

A Choice of Color

In Hokusai's print of the
Great Wave off Kanazawa

the sky is an extreme
refinement of the sea.

Its beige the color of clay
seems the perfect representation

of energy itself, a fineness of
texture transcending its forms.

And its electric stillness, like that
disclosed by awesome sounds,

has this feature of the sacred,
to make us feel when it appears to us

that it is in fact
we who have just appeared.

Message to the Pagans

nothingness the blank we
all come to in
death is simply the
possibility of anything at

all the beetling freedom
of the bird and
cloud the perfect freedom
to rise or fall

to explode like the
wave or form like
the slime mould more
and more disagreeing with

Baudelaire that there would
be anything remarkable in
creation out of nothing
one passes through the

heart of the cloud
of gnats and they
collect again silent in
the soft Homeric air

Ars Antiqua

Music less of passion than of number,
combining the beauty of water flowing
with that of exquisite masonry.
The leaves of the pecan trees outside
her window shudder in the warmth
of summer evening. Among them
the power lines disappear. Through
their dark silhouette is the red of
an old car on the street, a faded
Pompeiian red, not quite the shade
we have chosen for desire.

After Leopardi

Gracious moon, to remind me
(it is almost a year since then)
how I climbed this hill in anguish
to see you,
and you were there, alone,
above the wood as now,
brightening all.
But your face was in mist then,
and trembled from my tears
so troubled was my life,
and is, nor does it change, fair moon.
Pleasant is youth, when hope
remains and memory is small,
and one will think on
sadness and pain because they
seem precious still, believing they are but
the shadows that make life complete
and whole.

Danaë
AFTER SIMONIDES

When the wind rose
and the waves tossed her in the
carved chest, she fell back
and in tears
put her hand to Perseus
and said, "How much I suffer,
but you sleep.
Like an infant, in this
chest that shines in the night,
you do not see the deep surging
or hear the wind cry
with your face so beautiful asleep.
If what is terrible
were terrible for you, you would
open your soft ear to my words.
But sleep my child.
And the sea sleep, and this
measureless suffering.
May you grant some change,
Father Zeus, though forgive me
if I speak too soon, or
ask what is not my right."

Swallow Song
AFTER THE ANONYMOUS GREEK

Again she comes
again the swallow comes
bringing the hours of beauty
the years of beauty
on her back like night
on her belly the color of stars.
Open your house
and give us cake,
but even bread will do
for the swallow disdains nothing.
Shall we go,
or will you treat us?
Good if you do,
but if you don't
we will never let you be.
We will unhinge the door
and take your little wife
easy enough to carry away.
But if you do
give us something big.
Open
open the door
to the swallow,
and give us something big,
for we are not old men
but children.

Baucis and Philemon

There was the moment
of fear when they
recognized the gods.

But because they had
understood the coolness
of their room and taken

in the strangers,
the gods gave them a life
that would bring

with no more labor a
shade to the season
of unbearable heat.

Poem

one sees the budding of
trees it seems always
two or three days after it
begins, like awakening
from a sound one did not
actually hear

Ode, Garrance

Or, the world is our guest. Garrance
in Baptiste's room that night,
the moonlight behind her, she having
wrapped the sheet around herself,
his back turned out of modesty,
offering herself suddenly like
an Indian goddess, though neither
puzzled nor disdainful when he
fails to find how to accept her,
a seed trembling in the autumn wind.
She knows she has entered his heart,
that he leaves out of admiration.
So she sleeps in his room.

Monet

*Painting (and you paint what
you love) takes away desire
of possessing things.*

Lorine Niedecker

images over which
we have no
control signum of

humility where Lorine
does your boat
on still water

go even there
went his hand
before the canvas

and its colors
the circle of
flesh held to

the folds of
light their histories
how then we

say we are
free because we
know them haystacks

the colors of
Paradise will we
wait each time

we do not
see for the
eye comes as

it will and
would be nothing
in our determination

flame of seeing
and through him
we breathe the

incense of its
burning by what
measure are his

waterlilies unreal beyond
our control waiting
to be seen

Debussy

from Greek times
not the fawn
of the deer

but the one
of dark and
sleepy eye where

is neither the
grey of age
nor of mist

but the shade
of resin that
catches fire and

softens with the
sun follow him
into the shadow

where the light
is more clear
and if he

accepts you he
will play the
flute before sleep

Monet at Giverny

In a photograph he stands on the Japanese
footbridge, as on the bridge of dreams.
One reads only a little in his life
to see with Kant that "civilization, even
in its perfection, does not ensure happiness,
but only brings us to test and prove our freedom."
He and his family were "impressed with speed,
and would often go to the car races." He could see that
technology brought a certain nuance to things,
they had begun to coruscate in another space,
the space of invention. Painting for Monet
was not an interrogation of Being,
but engineering. (His triumph was to have
shown how largely fear is beside the point.)
And so it seems fitting that he stands on a bridge,
his canvases proposing, as they span
the depth with light, how Socrates' soul
might have crossed into Agathon's body,
or Plato's star joins the living with the dead.

Paris

Although it trills on with endless
reverberations, for all its grace,
is innocent of glamor.

the Wen fu *of Lu Chi*

The floating cloud
that was the city of Paris,
city of theoreticians,
city of Baudelaire's long walks,
and Proust's small room. Its young men
were like old women, for whom
the world was not quite to be believed.
Their virtue was to be refinement,
and yet they did not care to be innocent,
not altogether innocent
of glamor.

Parisian Rondel

Bring us through the winter.
But whom are we speaking to,
what spirits without or within

that leave us to our own
in spring? New flowers the
color of blood and sea

weave together earth and sun
and we cannot accept
their mystery, to believe

we are in their hands.
But bring us through the winter,
and we will stand on our own

unbelieving in spring again.

From the Forest

There are of course the eyes of
the lemur at night fixed by the
spotlight. There are then the dreamy

eyes of the orangutan as they gaze
into the richness of some sunlit
hibiscus it holds between its fingers.

The lemur must want to know where
the light itself comes from. Though
the orangutan, with its tilted head,

is like a drunk man whose mind
has come to rest on some single
feature or quality of things,

like one for whom the question
has become infinitely more pleasing
than any possible answer.

Photograph by Kertesz

Perhaps it is because they are of stone
the workman sweeping this drained fountain
does not notice them,

the sea nymph and river god lying together,
she awaiting his kiss, which he
delays, to take in the beauty

of her eyes. And yet the workman has been here
so often, doing just this, when it
first begins to cool and the

leaves fall and clog the fountain.
It is the same grey day each year
and he must wear his cap

and light coat. And there they are,
absorbed in themselves behind him,
stained perhaps a little more

with the year's rains.

Photograph of Bonn at Christmas

Along the snow-covered foreground
temporary stands have been set up
to sell fresh fruit for the season.

Their burlap awnings cast deep shadows
beneath the grey sky, but the neat piles of
oranges, especially, show in the darkness.

Beyond, the neoclassic façades
around the 18th century square
with its obelisk at the center

recede in the air dense with winter haze
to become pale, and if modest,
not without a touch of grandeur

above the holiday's makeshift scene.

The Snow Leopard

The question is
how often does it allow one
to see that it sees one.

I have never seen it in a
photograph that it was not
returning the camera's gaze.

Unlike Susanna and the elders,
or Hylas pulled under by the nymphs,
this creature of the snow

will never be taken by surprise.

Atget

There is this photograph of the
Parisian whore sitting outside her
apartment. She is petite and plump,

and holds one hand to her face,
her forefinger impressed upon her cheek,
her eyes averted from the camera.

There is on her face a wistful
and almost embarrassed look,
as if she were fretting.

Like a tiny bird for its egg
she argues with nothingness for at least
this possibility of shame,

and nothingness, being never one to argue,
and seeing no way to convince her,
in her averted eyes concedes.

Spinoza

He looked long at the world
as the door behind which he became imprisoned
in his mind.
                But because there was
a mechanism, he finally unlocked it
and then carefully swung it
completely open.
                There he leaned with his
back against it, its meaning now
subtly transformed, his heart throbbing
freely, and eyes at last closed.

Breton Landscape

he speaks of
the horse of
pride he keeps

in his stable
when he can
buy no other

he ate well
at his father's
funeral like his

countrymen and hopes
his son will
do the same

Ma Mère L'Oye

At some point they try
to retrace their steps,
only to find the bread crumbs

they left so carefully
are gone. As only we know,
little birds have eaten them.

And if the story ends happily
it is not without the children's
having to face this misfortune.

But are we meant to realize
that if they'd known
of the little birds' pleasure

they might have despaired?
Or are we meant to perceive
that we live in two worlds

at least, the child's world
of lost ways, and another
we might call the bird's world

of unexpected feasts?

China

the extent to which it is
private

the world, in which we learn
to cry

a phenomenon, to
wake from crying and find

no tears, but the
chest

still
tight with pain

Hasidim

we will never transcribe
the stillness

or the silence,
one's shadow

mixed with the shadow
of leaves

a bird
with no sound to its wings

penetrates the leaves,
disturbing

not one

Psychopomp

sensuality in the
weight of bone

the beautiful parenthesis
of the dawn and

evening moon
the old are

sails that quiver not
taking the full

wind because light
is mineral

there is a hole
in the eye

Two Poems in Autumn

Who could express total extinction?
                                    Han Yu
The literal meaning will contain all the others.
                                    Aquinas

I

evening star and sickle moon
drive light deep into the heart
the nerves cover body

like a net of fire, the brain
is fire clinging to what the eye sees
even to this darkness

this is the season before the blind cold
of winter, voidlike dusks
reveal the treasure for a moment

how explain time within time
or unfold sadness within sadness
how travel far from hearth

when wind soughs through dry grass

II

cuneiform of the autumn hills
the sun having just set the moon
having just risen like a balance

I have awakened from my dream
of wonders in the sky
and walk beneath the trees
in the shadow of the earth
to recover from such deep feeling

did they happen I like Wittgenstein's
man who dreams of rain
while outside it rains

words perpetuate the notorious
but even they
will one day wear
into indecipherable form
like ravines

The Sun in Winter
AFTER TU FU

Flower
cold among the leaves of heaven.
And rock under water and stained by water
like the leaves of heaven,
impassive
to our need,
the withering need of ghosts.
My thought withers among the hissing waves.

Trace

If a star were a man.
If a star is a man.
Such power. I have tried to
imagine all the space that

is not the star. A man
sees what is near him,
the beginning of his absence,
its trace in his mind.

What is a fanatic
other than one who
has tried to reclaim
all he has lost.

The Rock Garden

The rock garden touched with snow,
the furrows
of the gravel sea filled with whiteness.

Is it an irony that these rocks
resemble islands,
for islands are not so carefully
placed in their sea.

His absence. Man
would be the being
that inhabits this.
But for the moment
such beauty is enough.
He withdraws his cup.
For the rest
there will always be
enough time.

Soon It Will Be

soon it will be for us
the silence of a winter night
we do not resist then

the body, but like a
quiet rain over land flow
into its ways

and at length will become the scene
of its will,
the sea to its tiny bark

An 18th Century Motif

Framed from a hill by trees,
a view of Prague
in the time of Voltaire.

From this engraving one sees
the city of man in some sense
still prefigures distantly

the City of God. In this
presentation it is as if the leaves,
like clouds, had parted

to permit one's gaze.
But in the pattern of roofs,
like a massive, irregular crystal,

one also sees the city is
no longer the clear image of
man's will and intellect,

but is indeed nearer a
mineral-like accretion. The times
have begun to look, more

than to justification, to origins.
And one returns to the image
and can only note it,

the silhouette of church and palace
graceful, eliding
the movement of thousands below.

Divertimento

For the moment at least we won't worry
about the implications. Older, passionate,
of excellent name, she has fallen in love

with a somewhat younger man of uncertain
means, who knows neither how to
acquiesce or refuse. The affair would be

comic except for the seriousness with which
he takes her. He is of course justly
not without suspicion, although suspicion

is a price he does not really want to pay.
This is in fact precisely what she
finds a little preposterous but also

so desirable in him. He comes to feel
he must never apologize to her because
it would humiliate her. Whereas she

is certain she has made him feel
hopelessly inadequate. They end up
writing each other delicately disguised

letters of friendship in which she feigns
approval of his uprootedness, and he
feigns devotion to her code of manners.

There is the right period of silence
between their communications so that
his interest remains genuine, though she feels

he is nevertheless ultimately confused.
And obviously as to whether he is confused
is where our interpretation, should we

have one, would begin.

Huntress

the crescent moon
her crown who
disdains the game

of love yet
there was one
whose pleasures were

his own who
had seen her
without looking again

She Has Waited

it is an evening of autumn
she has waited
and the stars have appeared

but now
content to be alone
she returns to her mirror

How Their Fingertips

less and less willing to ask
what do I want

more willing to let the story unfold,
tell itself, as they say, if it is a story

as in his painting of Ruth and Boaz
the bright, vibrant fields of grain
seen from beneath the shade of trees
Poussin seems at last

to have forgiven himself for being
forever tense

tense enough to notice how their
fingertips touch as they pass
the wine around in the shade

the animal seeks its consolation
here, within arm's length
all that is permitted between us

served our food
we move a few feet apart
and talk quietly

Good Luck

good luck
now the cricket comes

spring's meaning in the first
warm stone

the new buds turn the veins
of shadow into lace

perchance a bird
flashing sunlight

even the dogs
obsessed through winter

have a new gloss on their coats
and now like the rich seem

carefree

The Minor Risk of the Snail

hearing the mockingbird faintly
through the closed door

when I open it the full sound
in a very fine mist

dark morning in spring
the steps are damp
and I must take care as I
go down them

I take off my glasses
and do not put up the umbrella
I a secretary and bachelor

practice the minor risk of the snail
drawn out by the dampness

in my veins

Mother of Eros

by way of explanation
a lovely woman walks
by with bells on her ankles

and I a little drunk
here on the streets born of her
breath, Venus

well-wisher who visits us
thus with the small flowers
on her shawl

barefoot

Wind

cafe outdoors tablecloths
blowing and the
palmettos along the

fence she has
set down the
pot of coffee

the cup the
frosted glass of
water the little

paper containers of
cream the spoon
and on the

paper napkin fluttering
to hold it
down the change

Music

What is there to say of music?
The winter sun
through the window

fills my basin, putting
a faint light on the ceiling
and on my face

as I look into the mirror.
Or, suddenly I'm surrounded
by children

playing,
still too young to
join hands on their own,

and yet not so sincere
they would disdain,
unless forewarned, this

habit of the Muses.

The Garden in Winter

Birdprints in frost . . .
to have heard music.

Strictness against the anxiety of spring.
Only what is

contained will remember love.
From bareness

more light enters the garden.
Not all things

but elation as the old
count birds

or wait for dawn.
There is no other;

pool sparkling in
cold wind

is the mind of God,
the waves' shadows filling brightness.

November 7

Today lovely low clouds with soft
grey underbellies, the grey almost
matching the blue of the sky.
Like Vermeer's *View of Delft*,
patches of sunlight moving slowly
across the city. There is such stillness
one notices time itself; some
would say "time stood still,"
like the women in Vermeer's painting
who stand near the water talking
though they are too far to hear.
There is less sunlight than
shade today; one sees it it seems
as in the painting
always on distant rooftops
and trees. A good day
for reading at a window
or beneath a tree, the light
shining at the edges of the clouds
and from the small open areas of sky.

The Perfume

"Love is so simple."

Children of Paradise

At first the perfume annoyed me in the
restaurant. But then I remembered its
sweetness was a deep symbol to my
grandmother, who died after nine years of
gradual heart failure, and was a diabetic.
Life for her became both sweet and dark.
I remember how until I was ten
she would let me sleep in bed with her;
I would warm the soles of my feet against
her legs, and stare into the darkness
of the ceiling, or at the moonlit
window. And how she spoke of certain
things as "exquisite," the colors of
sunset, or a vase. And how one day
in the brightness of her kitchen she
put the tip of her finger into the
forbidden honey, and then put it into
her mouth smiling and almost winking
at me, showing me how to do the
same. And it seems now that
who stood before me then was indeed
none other than Eve herself, alone and
dying, trying to find some companionship
in her old argument with God.

A Photograph of Zapata

How describe his eyes except to say
they seemed on the verge of tears,
and yet also filled with resentment

and anger. They were the eyes of a
very young child, the eyes of determination.
But the mystery is that they were

also his eyes, an older man's eyes,
introverted, sad, almost blank,
that did not know what to do except

die making the world right for this child
within him. For no amount of reasoning,
no amount of apology would be

understood. This is of course fate,
when the child's determination conquers
the adult's words, for good or for ill.

Paideuma

At times I have seen the moon
that it had the beauty of a young boy
just learning the mystery of being seen,
full, low in the east, above the horizon
dark like the eyelid of a courtesan,
its yellow whiteness the color of sand.

The Father

The father speaks to his son.
He does not want him to be so
cautious. He wants him to roll

with the times. Later he will pay
for him to have a whore,
to cure him, as best he can,

of guilt. He wants his son to
survive. He has heard of course
the unexamined life is not worth

living. But he himself has never
claimed to be a profound man.
And once when challenged

by his son that he was not,
he made his stand with silence
and a look on his face

the son will never forget,
the rage of the one who gave
the accuser his chance.

La Règle du Jeu

*We decide nothing; but we are
responsible for the universe.*

Magritte

Shall we take on then
the nature of the father?
That time he will refuse

to feed us, that day we might
refuse to feed our children
because we will die

and want before then
to know they are
more than our images.

It admittedly says nothing
or little of the world,
which is the same

whether we end staring
at "the fruit rotten
in the serpent's mouth,"

or distinguish the dry
and liquid notes of birds
above the delicate fissures

and subtle inclinations of pavement
we walk along indeed
as if we decide nothing.

Sainte
AFTER MALLARMÉ

Pale, her viol
having lost its gold,
she holds the old
unfolded book that shone

once at compline.
The windowpane
is verged by the harp
the Angel made

of his even-flight
to her finger, poised
as it is above
the instrumental feathers

to caress them.
But she refrains,
such their iridescence,
Musician of silence.

Sacred Love

A thousand birds take flight beyond
his window. He lingers
for a while, curious at last

at the growing design
of his own aloneness,
like the evening light that brings

to darkness the birds
now alighted in trees, ruffling
and preening their wings.

Figura

more or less the same
as when I saw my
first love given to say

it now and ultimately
to worship the
dew sparkling on the wire

fence I saw her through
the trees there
have twenty seven years

later grown to
shade trees that
were then no taller than

us five year olds
our passion was
gathered from the air by

our small bodies my
fingers in the wire fence how
else did she know so

young to pass by
as if I were not
there

Nothing to Terrain

nothing before one
but the beast
that is oneself

asleep in its
magical dream and
the story goes

that one precipitates
oneself into this
dream as the

simple person one
is with a
name and history

and only then
one begins to
learn the terrain

Prelude

portrayal of the
sea parents early
bring their children

to see it
the odor of
a body and

perpetual wind it
is the living
little things scurry

at its edge
but do not
leave this breathing

jewel admirable if
you care for
time at all

Delicatessen

if serious animated
the Jewish face
ignoring the evening

beauty yet matching
its fullness complain
to God who

else the good
old days fresh
fish the pastries

in Florida are
out of this
world she laughs

knowing it means
something perhaps not
much but something

Texas

a court four
palms high walls
of glass and

pale stone the
narrow pathways meet
at a fountain

it is plain
without ornament or
figure its trickles

resound delicately along
the walls a
Moslem influence to

honor and enhance
so modestly the
sound of water

Rime

light rising in
the east isolate
beauty come here

where you can
see it the
admirable space between

dark buildings dark
trees mortal edge
of the moon

in a field
tonight the lovely
tree cut down

the fresh wood
a pale disc
like the moon

The Moon

several times I
came to see
it through the

branches and leaves
of a pear
tree now gone

perhaps a story
how we two
remain the moon

and I dependent
even more on
each other now

The Greek

how will we
identify the moon
above the sea

selene her loneliness
a task of
syllables gathering their

delicate life from
another realm than
that of time

she is there
we are surprised
betrayed into thought

Measure

Over the cafe
door a painting of
cockatoos

and fruit-laden
vines before
a misty dawn

in Malaysia.
It is the confusion
of delicacy.

We do not know
where to go;
nothing seems to lead

away, not even
catastrophe.
As when we first see preserved

in clay the
dragonfly's
broken wing,

or an atrium
in Pompeii,
with its honey-like

light in the afternoon.

What Is This Now

Boy with long hair,
writing.

His hair falls down
beside his face as it

would if he were
above a lover.

Why does he
write? What is

this now so
private to him? What

is it that has
the appeal to

close off all
but this written line

on whiteness?

Young Master

Sappho said of the evening star
that it draws back together

what day has dispersed. Goats,
the goatboy. Thinking perhaps

the night is an infinite design
we can only sleep to.

For what is there by day
but the gentle and timid will

of the goats. And the goatboy with
his staff, learning to follow.

Vermeer's *Woman Asleep*

It might be taken
as a symbol for
Western art, this

sign divesting itself of all
appearances it is
a sign.

Here we have a woman
asleep among the objects
of her household.

The point is of course
in this record of
beholding her to be

as unmannered as possible.
Which is not
to assert that

one takes no point
of view. It is rather
like the matter of

sleep, which is never
learned. The point of view here
does not reveal,

it merely encounters
the curious arrangement
of this woman's mind.

The Roman Portrait Bust

It is after all not self loathing but
mild self contempt that she feels.
Only some vulgar conversion

would change that.
What she fears are the Eastern religions
that make of the world

she knows a brutal fantasy,
no more than a stage
on which everything plays its

part, down to the mindless
flowers. So that it is to her
ideal though by no means

a creed when she teaches
her grandchildren that because
we do not altogether matter

to the gods, they need not altogether
matter to us. It is her instinct
that tells her outside this

notion the very act of breathing
takes on the ominous tone
of unconscionable pride,

or worse, absolute submission.

Casanova's Mother

FROM THE 18TH CENTURY SWEET LIFE
BY FELLINI

The chandeliers have been extinguished in the opera house.
Casanova stands in a silent reverie.
She has been watching him from her box since the
hall has emptied. At last she hisses to him.
He is startled, but approaches. Only to be
embarrassed when he discovers who it is, having
neither seen nor contacted her for many years.
A talk between them ensues in which she is unpleasant,
pointing out his neglect, but not overbearing,
and he is polite, but makes in fact no promise
to visit her. Her servants are late. She is lame.
So he carries her from the hall on his back, down
the great staircase, to her coach waiting
in the snow. The footmen assist her inside,
and the door is closed. In the moment or two before
she leaves, she can be seen through the frosted pane,
face almost indistinguishable in the dim light, making
some ambiguous gesture at her throat, adjusting perhaps
a jewel, or her collar. All that is unmistakable
is the glimmer. Already she is no longer thinking
of her son. And as her coach pulls away, he
almost calls after, raising his hand, having forgotten
to ask her address. But then he realizes, with a
faint smile, that not knowing it is perhaps his only
excuse. It is certainly his only revenge.

Ballad of the Beautiful Ladies
AFTER TU FU

With the festival spring
is truly here. Along Changan's winding stream
the ladies walk
looking proudly ahead, or for a moment
casting sidelong glances to each other
under knowing smiles.
Peacocks and unicorns embroidered
enhance their lovely figures.
About their heads flash
the colors of the kingfisher and pendants
of cut jade, about their shoulders the
soft glimmering of pearls.
Among their number are even
the sisters of Yang Kuei Fei.
At the banquet are served the
purple meat of the camel and
the white of raw fish
on crystal plates. But these
are hardly touched.
And though demons would be
moved by the music, all
await expectantly the greatest
to arrive. At last he comes,
triumphantly if indifferent,
on horseback: he alights
at some distance, and strides
through the catkins covering the
spring grass. A blackbird snatches
a red kerchief and flies away.
All know the power of Minister Yang.
They have been burned by his slightest
touch, as studied as his temper is
uncontrolled.

The Life in Art

Arachne
her hands, to which
Athena will assign no fate,

move about the loom
like points of sunlight on water where
the wind lingers

and though the goddess gives to mortals
a tale of pride
and skill that never ends

it is this she sees
the sun moving
to the wind

Ousia

Narcissus could not
move he beheld
such beauty but

Li Po liberated
by wine drowned
in the Yellow

River trying to
kiss its reflection
of the moon

Evening Star

old woman
to herself, sitting
elbows on knees
legs apart
the cigarette, the hands
unconscious but articulate
the brain having fallen
sixty years through the
abyss
she sleeps less
and eats less

Ontology of the Wind

Ortega y Gasset said
a restlessness,
as over Theognis' barren sea,
herder of waves,
in whose endless movement
is expressed his thought,
"If one's prison were one's home,
would one leave, would one
return . . ."

Erebus

One by one
they linger above Lethe,
trying to remember what had

been like this, so full of clearness
and movement and silence,
little suspecting that nothing

is more obscure. And so they move on,
for only the living are drawn
to perplexity.

Stoned

Patrick, Leonard and I dipped our
fingers into the stream reflecting
the evening sky. The supple V's
appeared barely wavering on the surface.
We went on then across the stream
one by one, carefully on the stones.

To Choose

the wind that if I could
choose to hear, though I do,
I would

Mother said
of that primacy
though it is only a word

that I would have chosen
what I have done
she who believes only

what she has done
and in that sense alone
heard the wind

seen the clouds of evening

From Tacitus

Only humility is endless.

                                        Eliot

It is twilight on the army in Pannonia,
and summer, the time of discontent.
The respectable have retired to their tents,
but the rabble remain.
A former applause-leader in the theater,
one Percennius, "experienced in exciting
crowds to cheer actors," stands on a mound
and exhorts them, calling up their hardship.
He speaks of "grim war and unprofitable peace,"
and ends pointing to the enemy's campfires
"actually visible" from their quarters.
What follows is a grand tale of mutiny. But one
notes here a remarkable detail. The respectable
retire at twilight. They will later make
good Christians. They will prefer
the light of day and they will hope.
But they will not aspire. For them only humility
will be endless. Of course Percennius and
the discontent know well, indeed all those
who love the stage, that humility becomes maudlin
the very moment it is acted out. This they have
a keen eye for. And so they remain, wanting
no part of humility. They are rather
drawn to the twilight, that soft,
alluring time when such men expect diversion,
for nothing else offers itself
but tasteless sleep.

Hard Labor
for George Oppen

It occurs of course to each man
that nothing transcends death.
But we know equally well

that something rhythmic and musical
has entered the very earth we
stand on. I remember seeing a mural

in an early Chinese tomb, of a
man and ox ploughing a field
at dusk. The field had a small

house at its edge, and the sparse
vegetation was marked by a brushstroke
here and there. This of course

took on a special meaning in the tomb.
Life has asked something of us, call
it labor, even hard labor. But the

point is rather than wondering why
we were ever asked at all, seeing instead
that we did answer, not just laboring

in the field, but painting that labor
in the tomb itself, and moreover
without glamor, painting

that labor alone.

Louis Zukofsky
d. May 1978

kind
note

to
mankind

there are
the words

the words
are there

as shadow corresponds
to leaf

so mirth
is reason

Psalm of Africa

lovely young
black man leaning
against the wall

on this clear morning
in spring with
your eyes half closed

taking in the sun
a cigarette hanging
from your lips

it seems you are
swaying inside
in your mind

like the sea
one can only
wonder to whom

you will first
speak when you
awaken from your dream

Alexandrian Idyll

What shall we say
of life's darkness
but with Theocritus

that we bend to the yoke of Eros,
leaves borne by the
lightest wind,

and that Hylas, the beloved,
was indeed the fierce Hercules'
prey?

We must take on at last
love's terrible identity
and hunt lest we starve

as we were hunted by love.

The Spring of Bandusia
AFTER HORACE

O Bandusia, as clear and sparkling
    as the finest glass, you surely deserve
    our sweet wine and flowers. Tomorrow
        you shall have a young kid sacrificed,

its forehead budding with new horns
    for a career of lust and battle. Yes,
    in vain, for its bright blood will
        stain then your icy waters.

Though the Dog Star rages you remain
    untouched by its corrupting heat,
    a cool pleasure to the wearied ox
        and wandering herd. You shall be

famous among springs as I sing
    the oak that shades your source, and your
    voice babbling among rocks, from which
        you so playfully leap down.

Soracte
AFTER HORACE

You see how Soracte
stands white with snow,
   how the rivers lie frozen,
     and the forests

can no longer sustain
their burden of ice.
   In such cold, one piles
     the logs on high

and brings out the Sabine
now four years old,
   Thaliarchus, and leaves
     the rest to God.

He alone withholds the
storm, and allays
   the cypress' moaning.
     Treat each day as if

it were a gift from him,
and ask no further,
   and let your youth
     bloom while old age

is still far away. Now
you should seek the squares
   at night, dance,
     and smile to hear

the laugh from some
darkened corner, where a girl
   so coy
     thus has her kiss.

1717

The Embarkation for Cythera
Watteau's haze of spring
poses of ease & delight

there shall be no complaint
no doubts only his arm seeking
to turn her to the path below

& her eyes which have been told
to take in seldom her love
then what else is there

but his whisper & her laugh
what else indeed will Eros endure
but Reason's fainting

to speak Love's name
& thus show himself ever the knave
for disputing Love

D'Orfeo

If you would be certain I am here
I will be forever lost to you.

Natanson speaks of Husserl's quest
for a radical certainty either in,
or of, or from the world.

I am a poet, not a philosopher,
and so delight more in
ambiguity than in certainty.

But let us say you wanted to be
absolutely certain that someone
loved you. It's not that you

would have to be willing
to be certain they in fact did
not love you, though you would.

It's the tests you would put them to,
the proofs you would demand
of them. Love would have to become

entirely a matter of the ingenuity it has in
proclaiming itself, like a man
who knew how to spend any

amount of money quickly.
But love knows how to spend
a penny well. And not always

immediately. Sometimes
never. As you can see I am accusing
Husserl first of a vulgarity, only then

of a fundamental error.

The Coachman's Dream

Voltaire
in a dream
showed me his factory.
The impression was a
brightness of chalk and pearl
and silver. He then
took me down a terraced
garden to the lake,
and there sat in a dark
niche of foliage. The dream
ended when I realized
he was waiting for me to swim.

Parks of willows and swans
are the powders of desire.

God has become so strange.
As a man I did not see
who saw my coach pass a bridge
and was pleased by the romance
of a coachman, and of the reflection.

To Mallarmé

The anvil keeps its secret
as the bird's shadow slips
across the terrain. Athena's eye
is the flowering plum

beneath a grey sky (there are
no bees, only a cold wind),
and wisdom's laugh is the sound of
crusht brightness. But those

who have read deeply after war
will borrow the maiden's
blush at any cost,
not because she averts

her face, but because she has
met her love as the seed
instils the fruit. And as
the sweetness turns to the tears

of Fate praying to herself
as she weaves her own doom,
you may hear the seed
grate against the teeth.

To Baudelaire

Only remember how
the most prized flowers
of the ancient world
were natural to hell.

And even in Dante, though
hell has despaired of
heaven, among the blessed
was brought the memory

of those things they
had abandoned. Even so
this stem was cut and
in the vase seems swollen

by the glass, and yet
supports the undistorted
delicacy of the petals
and leaves above.

To Roland Barthes

Where shall we go now?
Heaven withdraws before it can be touched.
To draw one's finger across one's lips,
the shape of desire, where one speaks.
To speak of bliss. It is to go from
man to man and find what he is
willing to say,
quietly expanding the circle of compassion.
One tries to construct oneself like
the deity (in this there can be
no blame) but one is imprisoned within
a paradise, and death, like the
step outside where one leaves one's
shoes, cannot speak. Nonetheless
there is this narrow space
through which many pass. One has
indeed lost count. Among them
a little titmouse the color of dust,
alighted for less than a second,
powerless but for its delicate flight,
therefore eluding all anger. Perhaps
this is you, my dear Barthes.

Light of the World

no my love
wait wait to
see the rose

opens only in
time and has
brought all her

knowledge into it
the knowledge of
wind and cold

Simplicitas Syntactica
for Stanley Cavell

Alongside Cervantes' "All affectation is bad"
on this literary calendar
is the photograph of a Moorish gate in Spain.

Through a thick medieval city wall
the gate affords a brief, dark passage
between the exterior and interior of the city.

The outline of the passage itself
begins without architectural comment
on the ground, and rises cleanly through the

height of perhaps two men
to a small protuberance inward, where it becomes
a circle that bulges slightly to a point

at its zenith, like a droplet of rain.
Before the gate is a shallow pool of rain
reflecting on the left the darkness of the

passage, and on the right the bright
sky beyond. To the left is a small
fir tree with its pointed silhouette (similar

ones can be seen through the gate along the road
outside the city). The gate
is of such simplicity that it

is readily enhanced by these, the pool
and fir tree. And one can see
how they, in themselves as simple,

might as readily pass unseen.

Tomb Murals of the Han and T'ang
for René Char

In reproducing these murals
the contemporary Chinese craftsmen
have carefully reproduced the blank patches

where the ground has fallen away,
or the pigment been eroded by mould,
or otherwise by time.

It is curious. On one mural a
blank patch extends across the face
of some official where he sits

collecting taxes, then across the
brushstrokes signifying the granary
he administers beside, and then on

into a blank area that had
apparently not been painted originally.
This is the careful reproduction

of a blank across a blank.
In this mode of attention there is
no speculation. One does not assume

even that nothing was there,
though completeness is of course
a constant temptation.

It is merely astounding
that this should seem more spontaneous
than deliberate. And perhaps the emblem

for this is very near . . .
the breath of fresh air that blows in
when finally a tomb

is unsealed.

On Hearing *The Musical Offering*

What is it that really concerns us?
Difficult to confront it within the
ambit of a poem. They say a poem

is artificial, a made thing, and
on the other hand that to find what
troubles us we would have to return

to the beginning of the world. Also
that beauty is a salve, as Campion says
a painted hell, if a poem deals in

beauty. And if beauty can only be
arranged, a kind of false staging,
is what we seek then a matter of

recognition, of belief? I am listening
to the music. A light wind comes through
the window, and the sound outside

of leaves blowing.
A strange labor has gone into all this.
One tries to dream of brute matter

over which miracles are worked, as if
the spirit did not have enough room.
But it is a futile dream. Things

are not so simple. A correspondence
has arisen between us and the
world, and we see that we might be

as consistent in our thought as it is
in its muteness. And that is what
concerns us. The world does not express

itself in words. Or rather more
accurately, its words pass unexpressed.
I asked if it was recognition or belief

we sought, and then felt the wind.
Say it had been night and there
had been a candle. The wind would have

filled the curtain and blown out the
candle, drawing a breath of smoke
through the darkness. Impossible

to say that nothing is there. And
yet we must refrain from saying so,
perhaps living for this very moment,

call it a perversity, or a confusion.

Begin Anywhere

Mu Ch'i's *Persimmons*
begin
where you please to

note these persimmons
you may
begin anywhere

they contain
no meaning but
their own beauty

which is in no
demand we may make
of them if

you are like the wind
silent unto itself
you may find a voice

in them

March 17

We talked of spring's first flowers
  by candlelight.
Outside beneath stars
  the wind blew through new grass.

First the narcissus with its small
  white clusters and pungent smell,
the fruit trees that are careless
  to bloom so early, the pecans

so cautious that will bud only well after
  the warm days have come.
My friend told me of a dogwood
  he had just planted, and so might not

bloom at all this spring. We talked
  of the iris, that comes for a few
days, and then is gone, so regal.
  I tried to remember Chomei's lines

on how the dead ride out of Eden
  on clouds of wisteria, no doubt
tipsy with its perfume.
  We blew out the candle

to roam through the garden, noting the
  dim outline of the crocus, and feeling
the branch of the redbud
  a day or two in bloom.

And Yet I Hardly Notice

we who have spoken of little or
nothing so well

if we could describe the iris
it would be almost as if
it did not exist

how shall I say, surprisingly one
has appeared near my door
and yet I hardly notice my
unkempt garden as I come and go

and yet there it is almost
as if I had planted it

as if one so ignorant of such things
could sufficiently care

Poem

I would be a mirror
to the flowers, no,

one could not lie about this
it would please them

though otherwise
it is a matter of indifference

they do not wait for me
they do not worry

that I might not come

A Certain World

Fantasy and practicality.
Terms of the horoscope
I have long admired.

Along with talk of
honey and ginseng tea.
Only half my friends

have lost faith with
the world. Should I say
to them their faith

is their good nature?
Grandfather took me
to hear the whippoorwill

and said nothing
but that when I was
as old as he

I could bring my own grandson
to hear it. The repetitions
of sweetness come naturally.

Think how each night Eros
came to Psyche.
And how a child

will hold a cricket
in the hand carefully
oh so carefully

until it sings again.

Postscript

a certain aesthetic category
in the Japanese Zen mind
the sadness that comes when
one perceives the extreme
naturalness of things

perfection is indeed the saddest
of all things
there is no compromise
none of that old come what may
war is the hypostatizing of it

when we look at nature
at the unaware
we reverse the order in
which we were conceived
by her, ours is the gaze

that seeks perfection
we are sad because thus
we have banished peace
from our mind, peace
which comes by the road